Communing With The Father
- *At the*
- *Table of the Lord*

Wayne C. Anderson

Copyright © 2016 Standsure Press & Wayne C. Anderson
All rights reserved.
Communing With The Father
At the Table of the Lord
ISBN-10: 1533412367
ISBN-13: 978-1533412362

NKJV Scripture taken from the New King James Version®.
Copyright © 1982 by Thomas Nelson. Used by permission.
All rights reserved.

Scripture quotations taken from the New American Standard Bible®, Copyright © 1960, 1962, 1963, 1968, 1971, 1972, 1973, 1975, 1977, 1995 by The Lockman Foundation. Used by permission. (www.Lockman.org)

Scripture quotations are from the ESV® Bible (The Holy Bible, English Standard Version®), Copyright © 2001 by Crossway, a publishing ministry of Good News Publishers. Used by permission. All rights reserved.

Scripture taken from the Literal Translation of the Holy Bible Copyright © 1976 – 2000 - By Jay P. Green, Sr.
Used by permission of the copyright holder.

DEDICATION

To the Father of lights I owe all and therefore dedicate this book, for without Him calling me up to Himself and showing me the place of His throne room, I'd never have known about this glorious Table Of The Lord.

To Patrick Graham Holloran, who left this earth in such a suddenly that creation seemed to shake. Patrick was my prophet. He said so, and I believed him. Three times he sat in front of me and said, "I am your prophet. Listen to me." I listen. Patrick Graham Holloran was a seer of and unusual kind. His love for people was extraordinary, and his place in the lives of so many will never be forgotten or replaced. I said to Patrick a year or so ago, "I'm going to re-write the Table Of The Lord book." He said, "That's a good idea, but don't change what you've done." So, this book has everything that the original had and more. Patrick loved the original book of the Table Of The Lord. He gave many away to people and loved quoting from it. Patrick was my friend, and I loved him like a brother. He was a "cutting edge" prophet of the 21st century who will no doubt be in the Book of remembrances of the great church leaders.

Patrick Graham Holloran
May 14, 1953 - March 16, 2016

Dedication

To Irene Joy Anderson. What can be said better than the scripture that states: When a man "finds a wife he finds a good thing and obtains favor from the Lord." (Proverbs 18:22). Thus, this writing and all the rest comes from His favor because of you. I am in love with you.

To my children of this earth, a father's heart is always dedicated unto his children. That is a law of heaven and earth. There is no accounting of the times my heart has been with you, and yet we were not together. The beginnings of the revelation in this book took place when you were small in stature and age. Now you are grown and have children of your own. This book is your inheritance. It happened when you were all in our home, living and loving one another.

To my grandchildren, I endeavor to accomplish the best for you. It is written that a "righteous man leaves an inheritance unto his children's children." It is my desire to do so with every spiritual blessing for you to take up in your walk through life, knowing that "you are the head and not the tail."

To my sons & daughters of the faith, of which I am more mindful of than they would ever know. "Did not my heart go with you?" Please know that I intend to leave a spiritual inheritance for you to walk in the authority of your faith and see mountains move and demons tremble.

Communing With The Father

At The Table Of The Lord

The cover of this book is another creation,
lovingly fashioned by:
Anita Lee Johnson

CONTENTS

ACKNOWLEDGMENTS -- I

WELCOME TO THE TABLE (AN INTRODUCTION) ----- 1

COMMUNION IN AN APOSTOLIC-PROPHETIC ERA -- 7

THE TABLE OF HISTORY -- 15

THAT SPECTACULAR NIGHT! ---------------------------------- 27

COME TO THE FATHER'S TABLE ------------------------------ 34

COMMUNION IS PASSOVER ------------------------------------ 45

PARTAKING OF COMMUNION ---------------------------------- 60

THE REVELATION OF JESUS CHRIST ------------------------ 67

THE END IS THE BEGINNING AT THE FATHER'S
TABLE --- 82

You can learn more about the ministries of
Wayne C Anderson online:

Standsure Ministries with
Wayne C & Irene Joy Anderson
Standsure.net

Our apostolic network:
International Apostolic Ministries
Iamtheway.org

Or check out:
The Emerging Kingdom
With Wayne C Anderson, Richard C Wilson &
Kevin Ford
Emergingkingdom.com

ACKNOWLEDGMENTS

In my acknowledgements I want to express my sincere love and gratitude to those who helped me in this work.

Irene Joy Anderson has not only helped me to experience the revelation principles of this book, but has been the necessary support system to learn and then to teach and then to write and publish it.

Anita Lee Johnson has been a faithful daughter-in-the-faith and assistant. She does so much more than just building the cover for this book. If I were to pen what she accomplishes for our ministries, there would be volumes recorded. She is tireless and a miracle worker. Irene & I thank God the Father for Anita all the time.

My brothers and their wives, Rich & Patti Carey, Kevin & Cynthia Ford, & Richard C Wilson. Together we lead the strong and growing apostolic network of International Apostolic Ministries. iamtheway.org

"I have earnestly desired to eat this Passover with you…" - Yeshua Notzri

(The Hebrew word "Notzri" means "Nazarene", a person from Nazareth)

Welcome To The Table
(An Introduction)

Welcome to the Table!

What table you ask? Let me tell you of a most magnificent heavenly place where in the middle of our Father's house is the splendid grand table that is prepared for us to sit and enjoy one another's company and where we can discuss great and mighty things with the Father our Creator, together.

There is a place that is reserved for you - at all times. You may call ahead if you like, or just show up.

How do you get there? Well, dear reader, it is a new and living way that is paved with the same substance with which the streets of heaven are also paved. It is the substance of the sacrifice of the Lamb.

Oh! Look, dear reader! Do you see? There is the Father's House and there in the middle is the great hall of His Table. Your seat is directly across from the Master where you can look into His glorious eyes. You can hear if He whispers. That is precisely what He wants.

As we look upon that Table, it is set and almost overflowing with a cornucopia of countless beautiful things. What are all these things, you say? Take a closer look, dear reader. These are the promises of the Father.

Oh! A Table set so elegantly with the great and mighty promises of the Father of all creation!

Promises to Israel, to us, and to the hosts of heaven. Oh, the promises, my friend, are so overwhelmingly delightful. Each promise has the effervescence of abundant life. Each promise is the substance of things long ago, in this moment and long into the future - as far as we can see.

These should in no way be considered door prizes, or an appeal to get your attention. However stunningly beautiful that they are, these are not decorations either. The Table is set with the promises of the eternals that mean your breakthrough can now be seen by you, dear reader.

This is our Father's Table, and we come to it as often as we want. All of us feel that we should be here more than we have been. There's only one thing to do about that. Let us come to this Table of communion more and more. Let us not forsake the assembling of ourselves together and let us rendezvous here at our Father's House, and let us now sit at His resplendent Table.

You see, this Communion Table is not a religious thing but a personal relationship. Communing with the Father through the Blood of His Son - His Messiah - is the most credible and efficient thing that we can do. This is never a waste of time nor is the time we spend at this Table unreasonable.

How is it effective you ask? It is effective in building our relationship with the King - the Creator of everything that was and is and is to come. It is effective in building our relationships with one another, remember that this is our rendezvous place. It is effective in presenting our case of injustice to the Just One Who will execute justice on our behalf. It is always effective in delivering us from bondages of all kind.

We have been told by our Host that we can bring our family and friends into this house so that they are protected from the judgment outside. This Table is for all; He has said.

Friend, I'm here not only to welcome you to the Father's House and to sit at His Table with you, but I'm also here to report the great things that He has done for you. I want to tell you of the importance of this Holy Place of Communion that can happen every day of your life, no matter what your culture or lifestyle and activities may be.

Dear reader, I have also been given the bidding to inform you of the intriguing history of the Father's deliverance of His children. You see, deliverance has always been integral to every aspect, every part and piece, every enactment of our Father's Table. From all that is evil in the world, the Lord of our salvation has redeemed us, and He intends for us to follow Him to remain free.

I sincerely hope you come to

understand that when Jesus (Yeshua), fulfilled the Passover, we were handed a victory that we should not let anyone take away from us.

Be aware that many have tried to take this place at the Father's Table from us. Many have needed to keep their controls of power over us and have tried to hide the freedom we have to enter the Father's House and find our seat at His splendid Table. Why? Perhaps because the evil forces against us know that if we freely rendezvous at the Table of the Lord, it will mean an end to the bondages and controls that they have placed upon us. We will escape their grasp and be liberated into the Kingdom of God's dear Son in such a way that the chains, the bondages, the slavery will no longer restrict us.

In this adventure, you will not be hearing the teachings of organized religion that has disabled us from partaking of our own personal communion with the Father at His table. You will not hear of the unscriptural fears and ordinances and theological nonsense that traditionally kept our liberty just out of reach.

Dear reader, you and I are His body and His Blood is for us and gives us the effervescence of life. We are reborn from above, and the Father of Jesus (Yeshua) is the Father of us all. You see, this is a family affair.

It is written that He took the bread and said, "This is my body which is for you..." and then, "This cup is the new covenant in My blood, which is shed for you..." You see, it is all for you.

So, please relax and read on. We are probably at a portal to your deliverance and freedom. It may also be the way of liberty for your family and friends whom you love. It has meant triumph to multitudes for millennia, and my sincere hope is that you will experience the victories that so many others have experienced.

Oh, dear reader, look and see... the door of our Father's House is already opened for us. The glorious light of His presence is shining from inside. The whole of His halls and His courts are filled with the activities of servant angels, and, OH, can you feel the welcoming Spirit of the Father that is bidding us come in and dine with Him? Yes, this is the rendezvous point...

So, Come.

Communion In An Apostolic-Prophetic Era

This is an apostolic-prophetic era or age. The Ecclesia[1] of Christ is awakening with tremendous authority.

Apostles and Prophets are now laying a foundation in the Church of Jesus Christ that will mean the greatest reformation that has ever been seen by mankind. Among the first of the reformational processes is the restoration of the "great doctrines of our faith." These doctrines are the spiritual weapons of warfare against the rising evil of our day. I believe you will find that of these great doctrines, the foremost, to be that of Christian Communion, the Eucharist, the Lord's Supper, the Passover, or that which I am

---

[1] In other writings I further describe the Ecclesia as the legislative body of heaven that manifests the will of the Father and His Kingdom upon the earth.

referring to as, "The Table Of The Lord."

The reason why I call this doctrine "The Table of the Lord" is because I feel that with the use of a biblically descriptive term we might unite all of the different theological approaches to this life changing and power-filled activity in our lives. What I would like to do in this book is activate the power of this grand Table in the reader's life! Though the place where this scripture comes from is actually a reproof, I can see that the correction that is prophesied in the book of Malachi will be corrected by our new regard for "The Table of the Lord." There is a need to bring clarity, purity, faith and courage back to our Father's Table.

Malachi 1:6-7
"A son honors his father, And a servant his master. If then I am the Father, Where is My honor? And if I am a Master, Where is My reverence? Says the Lord of hosts To you priests who despise My name. Yet you say, 'In what way have we despised Your name?' You offer defiled food on My altar, but say, 'In what way have we defiled You?' By saying, 'The Table Of The Lord is contemptible.'" (NKJV)

History has proven that in the intricacies and the complexities of this tremendous doctrinal truth we have been robbed of its root of pure and simple power. We have fallen to the traditions of man in so many ways. These traditions have made it difficult to celebrate the Table of the Lord in combined circles of fellowship and theological paradigms. Wait a minute; that sounds complicated in itself! Let me say it this way; let us come together and have a "Love Feast!" I simply believe that this is a more accurate description of the true Table of the Lord.

I will warn you ahead of time that if you have been even remotely involved with the Christian Church for very long, this may be just a bit disturbing to your mind. If, like all the rest of us, you have listened to the traditions of man for the biggest share of your Christian experience, what you read may either disturb you or excite you. I have even known some who have been annoyed at our forefathers of faith in their misguidance in the teachings concerning this magnificent Table. But please consider this – it's all a part of God's great BIG PLAN!

I invite you, instead, to have the great joy that's apportioned to you by the good news of Jesus Christ, Yeshua haMeshiach, and to know that this is a monumental season of the revelation of the Lord! For you see, "The glory of this latter house shall be greater than that of the former." Haggai 2:9 (LITV) It is just one of the grand patterns of the Holy Spirit. He tears down what currently is, to produce what is better.

It is important to realize that we all woke up today to an apostolic age. Apostles are on the earth today. Not only do we have apostles, but we have the teaching of apostles as well. In Acts chapter two, when the Holy Spirit fell, we see the people of God meeting in the temple daily, listening to the teachings of the apostles. "And they were continuing steadfastly in the doctrine of the apostles, and in fellowship, and in the breaking of bread, and in prayers." Acts 2:42 (LITV)

After His resurrection, Yeshua (Jesus), has been appearing to people for more than two millennia. All that have seen Yeshua alive are not apostles, but the leading apostles of this day have seen Him and have been instructed by Him. Thus, His kingdom did not dissipate after the first century but instead, "Of the increase of His government and of peace there will be no end, on the throne of David and over His kingdom, to establish it and to uphold it with justice and with righteousness from this time forth and forevermore. The zeal of the Lord of hosts will do this." Isaiah 9:7 (ESV)

You see it is all in God's plan. We are in the hour when there is revelation upon the doctrines of our faith. What I'd like to say here is that we don't want to blame our forefathers or the teachers that have been before. It simply has to do with the seasons of the Lord and this day of awakening of Christ's Ecclesia. Is it possible that the Lord might enable the waning of the power of His doctrine, so that He could raise it up with extraordinary power in an authoritative and revealing hour, in an hour when apostles and prophets are present, and the Ecclesia is arising? This is His plan and not ours, for "Little children, it is a last hour…" 1 John 2:18 (LITV)[2]

For those of us who cry out for the miracles of the ministry of Yeshua, Jesus Christ, here is what the Bible says about this: "And God has appointed these in the church: first apostles, second prophets, third teachers, after that miracles . . ." 1 Corinthians 12:28 (NKJV)

---

[2] "Little children, it is a last hour, and as you heard that the antichrist is coming, even now many antichrists have risen up, from which you know that it is a last hour." 1 John 2:18 (LITV - Literal Version by Jay Green)

Is there an order to God's Kingdom? Yes. Why does He seem to send chaos just when we begin to get our proverbial ducks in a row? It is probably because the row that our ducks were in was our idea and not His. The scripture clearly states that there is an establishing of apostles in the Church, an establishing of prophets in the Church, an establishing of teachers in the Church... Then miracles.

These doctrines are coming to life. They have meaning to us. I don't mean to go pseudo-theological with stuffy overtones that leave you in a cloud of despair, wondering what in the world I mean by all of this. On the contrary, you are going to find that this wonderful doctrine of our faith is quite simple. We just didn't understand it. We need the revelation of it.

Why do we have "doctrines" anyway? Why should we need them? Are they not just boring theology? What do they have to do with my everyday life? Although these are questions that most of us have when the subject of "doctrine" is mentioned, these and questions like these are based upon our weak traditional teachings that permeated our Christian experiences.

I think that we need some simple

understanding about "doctrine" before we go any farther. You may have heard the term, "doctrines of war" before and may not have understood the meaning of that phrase. Doctrines of war are military principles or a set of strategies by which an army generally fights. Although standard definition leans toward religion with this term, religion was not the reason why the Spirit of the Lord gave us doctrine. We have been given doctrine for militaristic strategies and principles. In other words, with doctrines we make war with the enemy for there is a war in the heavenlies.

The great doctrines of our faith are not much different than the doctrines of war. They are actually militaristic principles and a set of strategies. Doctrines are those established teachings of Yeshua, taught to us by the apostles of Yeshua, to wage war against the evil one of this world.

Since "For this purpose the Son of God was manifested, that He might destroy the works of the devil" 1 John 3:8 (KJV), there is, in fact, a war that we are all actively participating in the war in the heavenlies. Thus, Yeshua, Jesus Christ, the Son of God, has been revealed (or made manifest) to His apostles in this season, in this generation, to teach the militaristic principles and strategies of war that will defeat this evil one who wages war against the children of the Lord.

Now, you see why we need the great doctrines of our faith? When the application of these great doctrines are shown to us, we will put them to use and destroy the works of evil in our lives. They will defeat sickness, diseases, plagues, poverty, injustice and every wicked doctrine of Satan.

Further on in this book I am going to break a couple of theological rules that have been set down before us, as well as give divine revelatory bread from heaven. Please understand that these are severe days, and we need severe acts of faith that will deal with the evil that comes against us. Communion ought to be a fierce act of faith that substantiates our inheritance and positions us at the Table of the Lord.

The Table Of History

I'd like to reveal to you some of greatest principles of the mystery of Christ given to us as children of the living God.

Communion is communing with the Father, Yahweh (YHWH). Communion is also communing with one another. And, Communion exists as the greatest of protocols in presenting your qualified place for justice in the courts of heaven. It is a foundation of intercession that enables you to be set free from the grasp of the evil of this world.

You see, Communion is Passover. But, it all started, not in Egypt, but in the Garden with the parents of mankind - Adam & Eve.

Genesis tells us that Elohim (God) created the heavens and the earth in 6 really great days. I say great because He called them "good" but the Hebrew word is more of an emotional experience than just a label or description. Each day was very, very, good. But there was a seventh day that He also created which He did not call "good." He called that day holy. Holy means something like *especially awesome*. Of this seventh day, Jesus (Yeshua) once explained that He had not made man for that day, but He made that day for man. It was meant to be for man's pleasure and freedom.

On that sixth day, man was not created. Man was made. From the earth that was created, the Father formed man, and He did so in His own image. The Image Maker was fashioning His greatest work of all of His artistry.

There was a table of the whole of creation from which Adam and Eve could eat. Yet they were forewarned of the forbidden fruit that would wreck their whole house and put them into the bondage of the serpent and his code of evil. Eventually, the serpent set a great table before Eve and then Adam. This was the table set with all of the promises of the serpent and his code of rebellion. The serpent invitingly allured them to eat of his table - the table of falsehood.

But before all of this took place with the serpent the garden of the Father was luscious and filled with animal life and herbs and lush living growth and greenery.

Going ahead in time, all the way until now, the Jewish Shabbat (Sabbath), Seder[3] includes a small covered bowl at the table filled with herbs. This small bowl is passed around to each person seated at the dinner table on Shabbat, and every individual uncaps the bowl and smells the herbs and imagine themselves in the Garden of the Father when Adam and Eve were first free from the code of rebellion. It is a lovely experience to let the Father's Image Maker inside of us to sense the Garden of Goodness. Eden.

Eden was the best of all the tables. It was constructed, formed, fashioned, created, designed in the purest poetic and artistic sense. Eden was lost, but not forever.

Sometimes when I'm sitting with friends at a table, I like to tell of the many tables that were prepared by the Father unto His

---

[3] Seder is a Hebrew term for the order and organization of a celebration, especially the Passover meal.

special people throughout the ages. The tables that were eaten from by Enoch, Noah, Shem, Eber, Abraham, Isaac, Jacob, and the sons of Jacob.

Genesis records the foundations of our faith in the Father and Creator of all that exists. We are told in that great book of how Jacob wrestled with an angel and prevailed because of who the Lord named him to be. The angel knew of Jacob's name that was inscribed in the Father's extraordinary heart. His name was Israel (Yisrael). Israel (Jacob) had twelve sons who each became tribes.

Each son of Israel was the beginning of a tribe of peoples that would have the character given them by Yahweh in the Master Code of the construction of the House of the Lord. There is a beautiful and exciting story of the tales of these twelve sons of Israel (Jacob) in the book of Genesis. Let me simply say that they all ended up in Egypt where they not only prospered but Israel was arguably one of the greatest influences upon that whole nation so that they caused Egypt to prosper into the world's super power of that era. But as generations passed, the kings of Egypt, called the Pharaohs, change from generation to generation. Each new generation of Pharaohs and

Egyptians kept prospering because of the many children of Israel (Jacob). The Pharaohs got mean and possessive and very, very greedy. After four hundred years, the presiding Pharaoh saw all of the children of Israel, which eventually numbered beyond a million souls, as the slaves of Egypt.

The children of Israel were slaves in a land that was foreign to them. The Lord had promised a different land through their patriarchs, Abraham, Isaac, and Jacob (Yisrael).

Now they needed to be set free from the Egyptians who usurped ownership of them from the Lord. In other words, they stole the children of Yahweh, and that would simply not go unpunished.

Moses was chosen of the Lord to be Israel's deliverer. He and his brother Aaron went to the evil slaver Pharaoh and demanded that he let the people of the Lord go free. Pharaoh refused. The children of Israel were his slaves and the source of his prosperity and global power. He would, in no way, pull the power plug on his wealth and global supremacy. But he did not realize that he was not fighting against Moses or even all the children of Israel. He was battling against the Lord directly. All of this did not prove to be a prosperous adventure for the Pharaoh.

Israel belongs to Yahweh, the Creator of the heavens and the earth and all that is within them. No one will usurp the Lord's heritage from His mighty hands.

The same is true of you and me. We are His children, as we have been reborn from above and He is our Father. We do not want the code of rebellion to work in our lives in any way. Thus, we are purely and undeniably children of the living God.

Moses said to Pharaoh, "Yahweh sent me to you, and He says to you, 'Let My people go!'"

Well, Pharaoh wasn't about to do that, and he could've cared less about who Moses was sent by or for whom he might have been speaking. So, Moses was given ten national miracles to perform. Each one was seen and recognized as coming from the declarations of Moses, and empowered by the God of Moses. The first nine of those miracles were devastating to the people of Egypt but did not harm the children of Israel. Still the belligerence of both Pharaoh and the people of Egypt caused them to hold on to their failing grip of Israel.

I once saw a demonstration of a young monkey that was beside a cage with an orange that had been placed inside the cage. The monkey wanted that orange, so he reached through the bars of the metal cage and took hold of that orange. But the orange was too large to get through the metal bars of the cage. That monkey frustratingly held that orange tightly in his grip and just would not let it go. No matter what he did, he just could not enjoy the pleasures of that orange.

I think that the same mindset was upon the Egyptians. They could do nothing to keep Israel in their grasp. Yet just like that monkey, they would not let go of the object they desired - namely, the children of Israel. To no avail, however, they suffered by nine horrific miracles that impacted every Egyptian. They would not obey the command of Yahweh to free His people.

Then came the tenth miracle. (One might call it the tithe miracle.)

That tenth miracle was the Passover. Passover was the deliverance of the people of Israel, the children of the Lord, from their slavery and bondage of the Egyptians.

The Table Of History

The Lord told Moses to have the people go into their homes because their home is also His home. They are to set for themselves a lamb dinner. When they slay the lamb for their evening meal they are to take some of the blood of the lamb and put it into a bowl. They are to take a branch of the hyssop bush and use it to dip into the bowl of blood. They are to spread that blood upon the door frame where they enter into their home. Then they are to gather their families into their homes and have a lamb dinner with that lamb whose blood was placed upon the door frame as a marking to testify that the blood means that there is a lamb on the inside.

The Lord said that He would then pass over the land and any house that had the lamb's blood on the portal, He would see the testimony of that lamb's blood. Seeing the blood, He would pass judgment on that house as His own house. Knowing that if there is a testimony of blood on the portal, it meant that there was a lamb on the inside. This lamb in Egypt was a type and shadow of the Messiah, the Son of God. So, the lamb was judged as the Lord's kindred in that dwelling. So, if He sees the blood on the portal of the house, it means that there is a lamb on the inside.

The death angel that was sent with justice could not enter the homes of those that were judged by the Lord as His own. But every house without the testimony of the blood on the portal received the condemnation of the death angel and the first born of every womb was made lifeless. When I say every womb, I mean that no one in Egypt went untouched by the judgment upon their inheritance, from Pharaoh's house all the way through to even the cattle in the fields. This justice was against their inheritance just as they had wrongfully detained the Lord's inheritance.

The weeping and wailing was heard through the entire land of that nation of people. They suffered a terrible blow because of their rebellion, their greed, and their sheer meanness.

Now the children of God, the tribes of the sons of Israel, were set free to leave Egypt on a trek to the land that had been promised to them through their patriarchs.

The Lord spoke to Moses and told him to declare to all of the children of the Lord to never forget this momentous event of how Yahweh had delivered His children from slavery, bondage, and abuse.

Like an annual birthday celebration, this event was like Israel being born again, and the event of their rebirth was to be celebrated with a feast annually. Thus, Passover became an orderly celebratory feast that was part of the lifestyle of every Israelite, from that day until now. For more than three thousand years - Passovers - have been a central part of Israel's worship of Yahweh, Who is their eternal Father - their Creator.

Now, of course, this is a simplified presentation of an intricate real-life happening in the history of mankind. But this historical account gets even better.

Year after year, for more than a millennia, the children of God celebrated the feast of the Passover. There was order given and even added to, through the centuries whereby each dramatization would tell a part of the deliverance story and also prophesy into the future as a continuance of freedom from the tyrannical rule of that code of rebellion against Yahweh's inheritance. There was bread and wine and the lamb as well as bitter herbs and the reading of scripture, and more. All these were like props that dramatized the wonderful deliverance of the Father.

Then, (at the appointed time), came the Son of God, the Lord's Messiah. Yeshua (Jesus) was present and a participant of more than thirty Passover feasts during His earthly lifetime. The Jewish people have always known that the blood of the Passover lamb was their salvation. John the Baptist referred to Yeshua (Jesus) as the Passover Lamb when he saw Jesus (Yeshua) approaching and declared, "Behold, the Lamb of God that takes away the sins of the world!"

What a powerful declaration! This Son of God was what the Lord meant by the Passover Lamb!

At the end of His earthly ministry, Yeshua entered the upper room on that spectacular night, and everything changed. The Kingdom worldview of Yahweh was placed into operation. Oh, what a spectacular night that was, indeed.

The Passover was celebrated every year from that evening in Egypt, for more than fourteen centuries until Jesus (Yeshua) sat at the Passover with His twelve apostles.

The Passover meal, the Table Of The

Lord in its fullness, is now the revelation of Jesus (Yeshua) the Messiah of the Father. For we consider the testimony of the blood that was placed upon the doorframe of the homes of the children of Israel as proof. It was, and is, proof that there was a Passover Lamb inside. In the fullness of Passover now, we declare our faith in the Blood of Jesus the Christ (Yeshua haMeshiach), and that is our testimony of truth that the Lamb is on the inside of us.

Just think of how such an odd dramatization could bring about such drastic circumstances. Then, what might the Lord do with the Ecclesia today?

That Spectacular Night!

"Then came the day of Unleavened Bread, on which the Passover lamb had to be sacrificed."[4]

Throughout the centuries each year, the children of the Lord celebrated the Passover that had taken place. Most did not fathom the fact that the deliverance from Egypt in the days of Moses was indeed a prophetic statement - or promise - of what would take place on another spectacular evening.

Years, decades and centuries had now passed since that night in the land of Egypt where the children of Israel were captives and held in bondage and slavery to Pharaoh and the Egyptians. That great deliverance was to be remembered by every Israelite. Thus, it was remembered

---

[4] Luke 22:7 (ESV)

That Spectacular Night!

by every generation in every era that followed.

All this history culminated on one unsuspecting night. Oh, what a spectacular night it was!

The Rabbi Yeshua (Jesus), now in His early 30's, had accomplished all that the Father gave Him to say and do. This Passover was the reason behind it all. Everything previously promised was about to take place on this spectacular night and the hours afterward.

The Lord had prepared for this day, and everything was in order. During the day, Yeshua (Jesus) told a few of His apostles to go to a certain place, and they'd meet a man carrying a water jar. They were to follow that man to his master's house and the apostles of Rabbi Yeshua were to introduce themselves to the master of the house and tell him that their "Rabbi says to you, 'Where is the guest room, where I may eat the Passover with my disciples?'"

The room was ready for them just as Yeshua (Jesus) had told them, "And he will show you a large upper room furnished; prepare it there."[5] So the

---

[5] Luke 22:12 (ESV)

apostles made the Passover meal in that memorable upper room. (Powerful things happen in upper rooms).

Because the Creator began the creation of every day in the evening, the evening is the beginning of each day. So, the new day was about to begin. It was as though Jesus (Yeshua) was logging into a new day where the destiny of the world would be transformed into the Creator's vision for mankind. Yeshua (Jesus) entered the upper room and the world changed that evening - that was the new day.

"And when the hour came, He reclined, and the twelve apostles with Him. And He said to them, 'With desire I desired to eat this Passover with you before My suffering. For I say to you that no more, I will not eat of it until when it is fulfilled in the Kingdom of God, never!' And taking a cup, giving thanks, He said, 'Take this and divide it among yourselves. For I say to you that I will not drink from the produce of the vine until the Kingdom of God comes, never!' And taking a loaf, giving thanks, He broke, and gave to them, saying, 'This is My body being given for you. This do to My remembrance.' And in like manner the cup, after having supped, saying, 'This cup is the New Covenant in My blood, which is being poured out for you.'"[6]

When the Lord Jesus stated, "I have earnestly desired to eat this Passover with you..." He was not simply being cordial to His apostles. The words "earnestly" and "desired" were packed with high emotion and the tremendous thrill of having come to this particular moment in time.

Equally important are the words, "this Passover," in that, the Greek pronoun and article together give considerable attention to this particular Passover.[7] This Passover was not like any other Passover in history. This Passover was fulfilling all Passovers. Even the very first Passover profoundly prophesied of this spectacular night.

This is the Passover of all Passover's! The fulfillment of the Passover Lamb in the Kingdom of God!

We must not think that the word "fulfill" implies completion with no future. It is very western in thought and certainly not relating to the Hebrew. Fulfillment can actually be "fullness" but not completion or conclusion in any way. One might say that Passover is fully refreshed.

---

[6] Luke 22:14-20 (LITV) Jay Green's Literal Translation
[7] Literally reads; "this the Passover"

Passover was the precedent that all of the children of God can live by and close the mouth of the accuser of the brethren. It is the active proclamation that the Lord rescued His children then, and He will rescue them now. He delivers us in the past, our present and our future.

One of the most beautiful things about the fullness of Passover taking place is that when we see the early church (Ecclesia), in the days, months and years after Pentecost, they are celebrating the proclamation of the Passover deliverance at every meal time.

The apostle Paul even instructs the gentiles in the city of Corinth in protocols of Passover and the Table of the Lord.

So we now have the Table Of The Lord - the celebrated Passover - to rely upon in our lives now and in the future as well. It is an eternal promise. It is our individual authority to be free. Passover should be every day - every meal - even intercession throughout the day.

An even deeper look into Yeshua's (Jesus') words in this opening remark of this Passover was His words of passion. The phrase, "I have earnestly desired to..."

has two important Greek words that tell us of deep emotions that the Master is feeling, and He prominently describes to His apostles. The two Greek words would tell us of a burning passion that He is exposing toward His apostles who are seated at the table with Him. For centuries since the Lord gave the Passover deliverance to Moses and the children of Israel, He looked forward to the day when He would bring the fullness of this eternal deliverance power and justice to this very table in that upper room with the twelve men He loved and into whom He invested so much. And now they would take this deliverance power and justice to the entire world, beginning in Jerusalem and then Judea and then to the uttermost parts of the world.

I feel that it would benefit every child of God to spend much of their time reading and studying the happenings of this great night. This night extends from the dynamics which take place in that upper room Passover celebration to the Garden of Gethsemane, to the cross, the resurrection, Pentecost (in yet another upper room), and into the future of the Ecclesia (Church), that surrounds the earth today.

"For as often as you eat this bread

and drink the cup,
you proclaim the Lord's death
until He comes."

Oh, how this gives us a wonder-filled expression of His love surrounding us and protecting us. It tells us that our inheritance is intact, and we have the authority, as both individuals and as a united people, to decree our freedom from tyrannical rule and slavery.

"He was wounded for our transgressions; He was bruised for our iniquities; The chastisement for our peace was upon Him, and by His stripes we are healed." Isaiah 53:5 (NKJV)

Come To The Father's Table

Let us now look at the formidable work of the Lord's Table.

Since the beginnings of when I first became a believer, I have been a historian of the 20th Century revivalists, who flowed in the power of the Holy Spirit. I have found several common threads of experience in many of their lives. We can consider the writings of the revivalists like John Alexander Dowie, Maria Woodworth-Etter, Aimee Semple McPherson, John G. Lake, the Bosworth brothers (from Texas), Smith Wigglesworth, and the like. These men and women were all known for their passion for knowing the Lord Jesus Christ in a deeper and more intimate way. We must also note that all of these are especially known because of their miracle ministries.

Communing With The Father

As we search through their memoirs, we can find where most of them felt that God wanted them to take personal Communion with Him every day. A couple of them even said that if the power of God is going to be activated from within you to manifest the ministry of Jesus, you must sit at His Table often.

It is written, "As often as you eat this bread and drink this cup..." When reading this scripture, I have always questioned: "how often is often?" I think that "often" probably means more than just occasionally or just the first Sunday of each month, (which is common in many public church services).

When Jesus (Yeshua) sat at the Passover table with the apostles, He declared the fulfillment of Passover. When we speak of fulfillment, we must be careful not to throw out the importance of Communion with the Lord. Remembering from the previous chapter that there is a fullness, or, one might say that Passover is fully refreshed. So, we need to look with a bigger and broader view of what was actually fulfilled. Consider being someone who was appointed to "fulfill" a prophecy. I understand this to usually mean that someone prophesied and after a time someone did those things that were spoken or written in the prophecy.

Let me say that there ought to be a declarative stand in the hearts of believers when they come to the Table of the Lord. By this I mean that we are not just looking into a past deliverance but all of the deliverances of our future. When we come to the Table Of The Lord for future deliverance, there is a particular inclination for our worship at the Table to be prophetic or declarative and announce that our liberty is at hand. Thus, we do not want to "prophesy" incorrectly and nullify our freedom.

Now, in the traditions of men, here is where we find ourselves. Let us consider 1 Corinthians 11:23 & 24 (In the New King James Version and/or King James Version, which read similarly here):

"For I received from the Lord that which I also delivered to you: that the Lord Jesus on the same night in which He was betrayed took bread; and when He had given thanks, He broke it and said, 'Take, eat; this is My body which is broken for you; do this in remembrance of Me.'" (NKJV)

If you are reading from one of these translations, you should notice that the word "it" in these verses is in italics. The italicized word tells the reader that there is no supportive Greek word in the text and that the italicized word was placed in the verse to help with understanding, or for grammatical reasons. In this particular verse, the King James Versions put "it" in the sentence by traditional interpretation. (There are some newer translations that do not use the italics rule yet they still put "it" in the same position in the sentence for the same traditional reasoning. None of the Greek authorities or texts that I have studied have this important word. Most responsible Greek texts say simply, "He broke."

The reason for this is to coincide with the traditional Hebrew idiom that says "He broke" which is, therefore, stating "fellowship" and the hospitable distribution of the bread.

There is a problem with the old English translations that have set up much of our modern day theology for partaking of the Table of the Lord, which has to do with the words "He broke."

"To break" in this instance means "to hand out to everyone," as an act of hospitality and it comes through time as a full idiom that explains the whole act of being at a meal together. It does not mean "to break" as in something being busted, broken, wrecked, or kaput. In the Jewish traditions, when the Rabbi would "break bread," (or hospitably hand out the bread), he would say "The Bless." Perhaps something like, "Hear oh Israel, the Lord our God is One. . ." and in doing so, he would invoke the presence of God. Thus, the rabbinical purpose is to entreat the Presence of the Lord.

Herein is a more Biblical understanding of the "break" in the Jewish tradition. Now, unfortunately, the English word "break" has a much different meaning than the Hebrew word "break" used in this New Testament instance.

There is no problem in this if you look at it with the Jewish traditional understanding from which Jesus spoke. The word "broke" doesn't mean broken up; it means "to distribute" in hospitality.

Our problem has come by our misunderstanding of these literal words in our own cultural definitions. Because of it, we have Jesus saying, "This is my body" broken in pieces and busted up. He also says "This is my blood."

In contrast, He makes the act of the

believer's "Communion" a faith building prophetic drama! The partaker is invited to see the wonder-filled works of Jesus Christ performed before their very eyes and prophesied into being. Therefore, the picture that Jesus shows us is truly important and truly triumphant.

With Communion, we are making a tremendous statement. It is a remembrance and a declaration. It is, in fact, a prophecy. When you take the bread, you are prophesying! When you take the cup of the Lord, you are prophesying! In fact, every time you come to the Table of the Lord you are prophesying! And what is more; you are entering into the house of the Lord, sitting at the Father's great table, surrounded by His very dwelling place! Yet wait! There is still more!

Because the Table of the Lord is a prophetic drama, it is of great importance in each individual believer's life. You see, what I call a "prophetic drama" is the acting out a prophecy. And this is prophecy that will destroy the works of the evil one. It is prophecy that will speak forth the will of the Father. It is prophecy that will shape the future and the destiny of God's children.

Even so, the traditions of men have instituted strict limitations on how much of the Table of the Lord that we may partake which usually stops shy of the miracles that are needed to change the lives of believers.

We have even come to the place where, through the years, everybody knows that you are supposed to eat first and then come to the Table. We don't want anybody gorging himself or herself, so, therefore, we invented the little tiny cups and little bitty tasteless wafers that nearly choke every child in the place. (I'm sure that it was felt that nothing good for you could ever taste good.)

Furthermore, the established tradition is that we only do this in church, with what they call the "elements" handed out only by the assigned church officials. All of this may even take place only on the first Sunday of every month, whether you need it or not. (With the exceptions of a few special services like Christmas and Easter, as well.)

Although I am primarily talking about the church across the United States, this American-Western theology has unfortunately spread to the nations. All over the world this theological description has bombarded the churches so that there is nothing else.

"And he took bread, and gave thanks, and brake it, and gave unto them, saying, This is my body which is given for you: this do in remembrance of me.'" (Luke 22:19 KJV)

Jesus "broke" (in the Hebrew, Passover tradition) and then is quoted as saying, "this is my body which is for you." Most people misinterpret this as saying "broken for you."

In Matthew 26:26 (KJV) it says, "And as they were eating, Jesus took bread, and blessed it, and brake it, and gave it to the disciples, and said, Take, eat; this is my body.'"

Again, the italicized rule is still active. The word "it" is not in any authoritative Greek text of the New Testament. In this scripture, He "broke" in the Hebrew tradition pertaining to the distribution of bread, as as "we break bread together."

In Mark 14:22 it is much the same: "And as they did eat, Jesus took bread, and blessed, and brake it, and gave to them, and said, Take, eat: this is my body.'" (KJV)

So, in each case of the reporting synoptic gospels,[8] the King James says that "This is my body which is for you," not "broken for you."

Now, let's look at 1 Corinthians 11:23 – 24.

In the King James Version it reads: "For I have received of the Lord that which also I delivered unto you, That the Lord Jesus the same night in which he was betrayed took bread: And when he had given thanks, he brake it, and said, Take, eat: this is my body, which is broken for you: this do in remembrance of me."

Here again, the King James Version traditionally translates the scriptures in first Corinthians by adding the words: "broken for you." The New King James Version has followed the same traditional way of translating.

In comparison, the same scripture in The New American Standard Version, and some other study translations, place a few

---

[8] Synoptic means same, or alike. The synoptic gospels refers to Matthew, Mark and Luke only. This is because John does not have the similarities that the other three gospels have together.

more literal words to the verse, saying, "and when He had given thanks, He broke it and said, 'This is My body, which is for you; do this in remembrance of Me.'"

"This is my body which is for you." This is the toughest piece of scripture concerning the subject of the believer's Communion, all because of the King James Version, the traditions of the church, and the western theological mindset that was established by the church. They have placed the word "broken" into the translation causing a tradition of a breaking apart of the body.

Our problem is with the word "break" or "broken." To "break bread" and "break the body" in the Greek text are two totally different concepts. One means to hand out, and the other one means severed or fractured. The word "broken" isn't here in most reliable Greek texts of this scripture. The word that means "to hand out," or "distribute" is used in the original Greek Text.

All has been translated by traditional western church mindset and not the Hebrew of its origin. Jesus (Yeshua) did NOT "bless it." He blessed. Jesus (Yeshua) did NOT "Broke it." He "Broke." We have established strange Christian traditions on these mistakes and find ourselves doing things that Jesus (Yeshua) would never have done, and thinking we are doing what is correct and holy.

Communion Is Passover

The prophetic announcement of Passover is in Communion.

Because the believer's communion is the power of "the bless," the voice of the authority of the believer, the creative voice of the will of God on earth as in heaven, and the prophetic statement of what was and what will be, we are faced with another critical issue relating to the scriptures.

Let's look at Luke 22:14 & 15:[9] "And when the hour came, he reclined at table, and the apostles with him. And he said to them, 'I have earnestly desired to eat this Passover with you before I suffer.'" (ESV)

In our modern services of worship, we are not often taught that Christian

---

[9] We don't have this problem in Matthew or Mark.

Communion Is Passover

Communion is the celebration of Passover fulfilled. In fact, a large portion of the Church of Jesus Christ does not understand this important point.

The reasons and the rules for Passover are the same for Christian Communion. Jesus Christ gave the fullness of Passover so that The Table of the Lord in the Father's house is the victorious proclamation of Passover. What Passover did in the book of Genesis, Passover still does in the New Testament, as well as today. Or, you might say, "What Passover did for the children of God when they were in Egypt, Communion will do the same for the child of God today!"

The Passover – The Table Of The Lord is perpetual for all generations. Passover delivered the children of God out from under the bondage of Egypt, the hand of a heavy taskmaster, and it does the same for us in our lives in this era.

"And when the hour came, He reclined at table and the apostles with Him. And He said to them, 'I have earnestly desired to eat this Passover with you before I suffer.'"[10]

---

[10] Luke 22: 14 & 15 (ESV)

The words "earnestly desired" are very emotional. They could also be translated as "burning with passion!" This passion that He gave to this particular Passover is important. I often say that if you do not meet the things that constrain you with the passion equal to or greater than the passion with which they bound you, you will see little effect.

In the breaking of soul ties, for instance: In fits of appetite passion one will do those things that will bind their souls improperly. Because of passion it may or may not seem right at the time, even though remorse will set in afterward. The Table of the Lord is the way to their freedom. Just as Passover broke the ties that Israel had with Egypt, so the Table of the Lord is capable of breaking one away from the ties that bind. This glorious Table is about the regal and royal bloodline that has freedom, liberty, and divine health. If we only quietly sit and partake of this great Table with less enthusiasm and less passion than we had when we committed the acts of sin against God that have bound us, we will see little relief at all.

Jesus met this grand Table with a burning passion that would heal the halt and set the captives free. Should we not do the same?

Now, if this is a prophetic drama, let's take a look at it in this way. We have stood for years in the church and said: "This bread is my body broken for you." What are we prophesying? A broken body? No wonder we have Church splits, relationship splits, marriage breakups and general disregard for unity with one another. We have been prophesying Church and relationship splits for years. It was supposed to be a love feast. It was a gathering together, and yet we have been prophesying a broken body. The Church is the body of Christ, and it was not broken! It will not be broken! Let us say that with passion!

"Since it was the day of Preparation, and so that the bodies would not remain on the cross on the Sabbath (for that Sabbath was a high day), the Jews asked Pilate that their legs might be broken and that they might be taken away. So the soldiers came and broke the legs of the first, and of the other who had been crucified with him. But when they came to Jesus and saw that he was already dead, they did not break his legs. But one of the soldiers pierced his side with a spear, and at once there came out blood and water. He who saw it has borne witness — his testimony is true, and he knows that he is telling the truth — that you also may believe. For these things took place that the Scripture might be fulfilled: " Not one of his bones will be broken."

And again another Scripture says, "They shall look on Him whom they pierced."[11]

Can you see how we have wrongly portrayed the body of Jesus, by proclaiming that it was "broken"? Did He die in pain? Yes. Was He beaten without mercy? Yes. Was He pierced by the spear? Yes. Did His Blood flow to the ground? Yes. But was His body broken? No.

Every one of the acts of violence against the body of Jesus (Yeshua) is profoundly interpretive to the believer. Let us not destroy the victorious proclamations of the body and the life's Blood of the Christ with the traditions of man that will ignorantly declare the destruction of unity.

Because this is so deeply seeded into the fabric of the Church, I have had people get really angry with me about it. (Yes, we are talking red in the face, smoke coming out of their ears, angry!) So to help you with this great and powerful doctrine I'd

---

[11] John 19:31-37 (ESV)

Communion Is Passover

like to give you the witness of even more scripture on this subject of Christ's body. To do so, we will need to look at the Passover.

We find the Passover in the book of Exodus chapter twelve. This is the Passover, which was the beginning of all Passovers. It was a new day. In fact, every day at Passover is a new day – it is the start of a new day.

Exodus 12:46: "It shall be eaten in one house; you shall not take any of the flesh outside the house, and you shall not break any of its bones. (ESV)

That doesn't sound anything like "this is my body which is broken for you" does it? He has never intended for His body to be broken. You see, He wanted one body, one faith, one baptism. He has never intended for us to be declaring a broken body.

"There is one body and one Spirit, just as also you were called in one hope of your calling; one Lord, one faith, one baptism, one God and Father of all who is over all and through all and in all." Ephesians 4:4-6 (NASB)

Numbers 9:12: "They shall leave none of

it until morning, nor break a bone of it; according to all the statute of the Passover they shall observe it." (NASB)

Here in Numbers chapter nine, Israel is celebrating the second Passover. This was one year after they had been delivered from Egypt and were now on their trek to their promised land. They not only celebrated what God had done for them and the Table of the Passover, but they also prophesied of His continual power to deliver them out of the hands of their enemies! And to think, the Lamb was not to be broken!

"For these things were done that the Scripture should be fulfilled, 'Not one of His bones shall be broken.'" John 19:36 (NKJV)

John quotes from the 34th Psalm in his witness of the crucifixion of Jesus Christ. This Psalm has always been known as the Passover Psalm even though it does not mention Passover specifically. But when you read this Psalm and see it in your Communion you will, no doubt, experience the power of the Table of the Lord!

The 34th Psalm describes the miracles that can happen when you come to the Table of the Lord. I suggest that sometime you take a few moments to partake of the Table of the Lord and read this great Psalm while you do so.

We should begin to realize the afflictions that we get delivered from, (before they ever happen), at this great Table of the Lord! Begin to prophesy yourself right out of afflictions at the Table of the Lord! For this reason, I take communion multiple times a day if I possibly can. Before I come into a service, I try to come to the Table of the Lord. And, because "many are the afflictions of the righteous, but the Lord delivers them from them all," I get to watch the victory of Christ deliver not only me but the people that I minister unto as well.

This is such an important point that I usually try to make it very clear when I am teaching people about their personal communion. It is personal Communion (as opposed to corporate Communion) that will especially kick you up a level of sensitivity in the things of God. It will release you from the heavy handedness of Pharaoh: That is the sin, bondage, and the world's system. "Many are the afflictions of the righteous, but the Lord delivers him out of them all."[12]

---

[12] Psalms 34:19 (ESV)

Let us recognize that our vision of Passover should not be Cecil B. De Mille's version portrayed in the old movie "The Ten Commandments." He showed that green stuff was coming through the houses and going right over the households that had the blood on the doorposts. That is not the picture that the Bible shows us. The word "Passover" is a legal term. It is a judgment term. It is a term of judgment executed. It means that the hand of judgment comes upon this house, and the death angel cannot come in. It means that the claims of justice were paid for that household, and there is no payment due. Why? Because there is a Lamb on the inside.

How can the death angel come into eternal life? It is impossible. Just as East will never meet West. "Now the blood shall be a sign for you on the houses where you are. And when I see the blood, I will pass over you; and the plague shall not be on you to destroy you when I strike the land of Egypt." Exodus 12:13 (NKJV)

It is not the plague that passes over you but the judging hand of the Lord. He says, "I will pass over you!" Then the death angel will not have any legal right to your inheritance.

It is because of our need to prophesy correctly that I make this point. We are not to come to the Table of the Lord and prophesy the strength of the death angel. We are to prophesy the Lamb! This is not just semantics. It is our understanding of the great and glorious gospel of Jesus Christ. He has paid the price for our sins, and the bondage of the grave has been broken for everyone who believes. At the Table of the Lord, we are prophesying that great gospel of freedom into our lives! There is a Lamb on the inside of this heart of mine! Therefore, the death angel is not allowed to take away my inheritance!

Our inheritance even flows through time to the children that are yet to be born. Some governments are voting in full term abortion, and they have not the understanding that this is murder and requires judgment. We should not blame the people of that government because it is the Church who has the power to destroy the acts of the death angel. The Bible says, "If My people who are called by My name will humble themselves, and pray and seek My face, and turn from their wicked ways, then I will hear from heaven, and will forgive their sin and heal their land." 2 Chronicles 7:14 (NKJV)

Please note that this promise is unto the people of God, not the world. It does not say that if the worldly government will humble themselves and pray, etc. This is the act of the gospel being believed upon by the people of God, and it is God acting as their Father and giving them an inheritance in the land that no one else could have.

The Church must take up its responsibility instead of continually bad mouthing the moral issues of government. The Church is the target of the promises of God, and yet God so loved the world that He gave His Son to die for it. The question should then be; How many of those voters out there have we reached with the gospel of the Kingdom? If we get them born again, they will vote differently. We must take the responsibility because we have the ability to rely upon God's mercy and live. No one in the world can rely upon His mercy without becoming born again.

We can cry out for God to judge us. We can say, "God, judge me now because I don't want to be judged later." "Judge me; convict me, for I don't want to be convicted later." If I am guilty, I want to be found guilty now, not later. If I am guilty now, His mercy will rule and reign when I call upon Him. Because of His great mercy, we are here to win, not to lose.

When Passover took place, Moses was eighty years old. Pharaoh started killing babies when Moses was born. Passover ended all of that and broke Israel free from the cruel authority of a wicked enslaver. Passover brought about the end of an era. The same spirit is in the world today, killing innocent babies. Babies with destiny. All because of a cruel taskmaster of promiscuity and licentious living that masks itself as freedom. We need another Passover! I believe that we have that Passover in the revelation of the Table of the Lord. Our true freedom is found when we come to that great Table and see at Who's Table we sit. What power there is in the revelation of Who sits at this glorious Table with us.

Any Table comes about because of hospitality. Our Father has hospitably set a great Table before us. All we have to do is come to His Table. When you do, you will find a place that is always set just for you. We have a great need for revelation, and we will feast on that revelation as we come to His Table.

My prayer is that a report will come forth like the two who were walking along the road to Emmaus. They walked with Jesus, yet their eyes were prevented from seeing that it was Him, because they were without revelation. When they came to the place where they were staying, they pleaded with Him to stay with them, and He did. Their hospitality preceded their revelation. He sat at the Table with them just as He did on the night that He was betrayed, and suddenly, the revelation came to these men. Jesus! He was there all along!

They exclaimed that their hearts burned as He revealed Himself to them in all the Scriptures. I believe that we walk with Jesus in the very midst of our sorrows, and we don't know it because we have no revelation. Our hearts need to burn with the revelation of Jesus Christ in all the scriptures, and we too need to sit at His Table so that He might reveal Himself to us. Then we will find that He was there all the time. He walked right through all the troubles of our minds. Our blind closed minds.

So, let our hearts burn with that Holy Ghost fire from heaven as we see Jesus in all of the scriptures, pointing the way to our victory and salvation.

For you see, if you ever see Jesus, you

will never be the same. The manifestation of Jesus will forever change you. You must see Jesus, and you will see Him at His Table. Going to the Table of the Lord is not a religious performance or ceremony. It was never intended to be only a "first Sunday of the month" thing to do. It isn't a little bad tasting wafer and a tiny crystal or plastic cup of juice. It is our freedom. It is our liberty. It is everything that we live for. You don't have to know anything more than what I am telling you right now, and it will deliver you from all afflictions. He said so.

To partake of the Table of the Lord is to see Jesus. Therefore, it is the revelation. That is why He said that the bread is His body, and the wine is His blood. The Table is already set by the Father. You will see what is there at that Table. It is all about Messiah, Lamb, Lord, Yeshua (Jesus).

When I partake of communion, I like to use Matzo bread because it shows the Passover. The reason why is because it was made in such a way that there was no leaven in it. Leaven in the Bible represents sin. Where there was no leaven, there was no sin, and Jesus had no sin in Him. Secondly, it was to be pierced. It has little holes in it. Thirdly, it was to be broiled in such a way that it had stripes in it. The

Matzo will prophesy of Jesus.

Even though this is all well, I am not going to let an object (such as Matzo bread) be the revelation of Jesus to me. If I am without the Matzo bread, I will not be without the revelation of Jesus. If I do not have any Matzo or bread of any kind, I will go to the Table of the Lord with 7-Up and animal crackers or whatever is available. I do not do this irreligiously, but I work with my circumstances and use what I have in order to see Jesus! When He shows up, the circumstances change regardless.

On yet another hand, we don't want to be pride-filled in our supposed irreligious mentality about all of this. It is never good to be religiously irreligious. What is important is that we get to that Table and see Jesus. What I would like to have every time is Matzo bread because I can talk about it to Him. What I would like to drink, is the true blood of the grape, if I possibly can, because that is what wine is, it is the blood of the grape. That is what I want, but I will take a Twinkie and an RC Cola if I that is all I have. Again, the importance here is getting to His Table and revelating on Jesus, regardless of the products that are used.

Partaking Of Communion

To begin, I recommend that you get a big chunk of bread, Matzo crackers, or a bunch of saltine crackers and a big glass of juice. You might like wine with your communion, but I would suggest you not take your usual or daily communion with wine, at least not if you are going to take communion in the manner that I do, or you will find yourself on the floor, and it won't be the Holy Ghost. Now, I'm not trying to offend you about wine. It's time to get over all that wine stuff. I like to use 100% non-fermented Welch's blood of the grape – grape juice.

The reason is that I like to use a large re-fillable cup of juice, not just a thimble full like those little communion cups. There is a place for the little communion cups. They really are quite necessary when there is a large number of people partaking of Communion together. The reasons are not spiritual but logistical and strategic. Serving lots of people can be both expensive and messy. Little thimbles of juice or wine are less likely to make a big spill and are much easier to get to the crowd.

Some have thought this tradition to be something of a statement about gluttony, though. This just simply is not the case. After having read the scriptures would you ever approach the Table of the Lord with gluttony on your mind? No, of course not. This wonderful Table of the Lord is just too important to us. No true lover of God would ever approach this Table with the idea of filling their bellies. So, let us set that fear based tradition behind us.

Thus, small crackers and small Communion cups are for large crowds and that's okay. When we come to the Table of the Lord we can partake of His Table without being concerned about gluttony or misguiding our hunger for Him with hunger for food and drink. Whenever possible, we can use a larger cup of juice and a larger amount of bread so that we are staying at the Table for an extended time and revelating upon the body and the Blood of Jesus Christ. In other words, use however much it takes to worship, have intimacy and to even see Jesus. You can have as much of Jesus as you want. If you take small bites continually as you revelate on His body, you are sure to have a wonder filled experience. The same is true with the cup.

Now, my dream of Communion is to put me out in a hotel room someplace, or even a cabin in the wilderness, and lock the door and throw away the key. Just leave me with a few cases of crackers and a few cases of grape juice, because I will stay in Communion at the Table of the Lord the whole time!

This Table is about the revelation of Jesus Christ. He is the answer to every question and the solving of every problem. That which He accomplished at the cross has been enough to overcome every obstacle in our lives. We need copious amounts of revelation of Jesus. The more we see Him, the more we will see freedom and liberty. We are changed by every revealing! Change is the way of life!

Although I have never taken Communion the same way twice, I offer the following as an example of how I might pray and acclaim the promises of God at the Table of the Lord.

Communing With The Father

Taking the Bread and the Cup in front of me, I would pray something like this:

"Thank you Jesus, for coming and being so obedient to the Father. Father, I thank you for the body of Jesus Christ. He was wounded for my transgressions and pierced through for my iniquities. The chastening of my peace fell upon Him, and by His stripes I am healed. Every one of the lashes so violently placed upon Your body, Lord, was the name of every sickness and disease and congenital deformation that has ever come against mankind upon this earth. Each wicked disease and trauma is listed right there in each of those stripes. Beaten unmercifully, this bread, this body was for my benefit. Thank you Lord for this Bread – For this great body. It is the Manna that came down out of heaven. Thank you for this Bread. It becomes me Lord. You saw to it that it becomes me. This cup is the new covenant of Your Blood poured out, not spilled, but poured out as an act of Your will. Thank You for this Blood. This Blood cleanses me. This Blood cleanses my conscience from dead works. This Blood cleanses me from all sin. I don't have to be bound to sin this day nor this hour. This Blood is the glory that cleanses me. This body was not broken. Lord, I want to discern this body rightly. This body is one. Jesus, You died for this body, and I am passionately in love with this body. I discern this body as one. It is not separated and broken, but this body is one. And I am a partaker of this body. Thank You. It becomes me. You have seen to it that it becomes me. This body is healing. It is the covenant of healing to my family. For this is my bloodline. For this Blood is on the doorposts and the lentil of my house. And this house shall be called a house of prayer for all nations. And this house is a house of refuge. Yes, the righteous run into it and are made safe because His name is on it. Oh wow, the Door is Jesus. And I understand – I can see. I can see that this is the hand of judgment. This drink says that the Lamb is in here. This is the family of God. This is the body, and it is one. This says that all that I have and all that I am belong to You, Jesus. Without any reservation I am totally given unto You. Thank You, Lord."

This is not a rote performance. I partake of the Table of the Lord with revelation upon my mind each time. Many things have been revealed to me while I am partaking of the bread and the blood of the grape. In fact, everyday new things are revealed. My prayer is never the same, and there is continually new revelation of

Jesus that is given to me.

You see, if I have found that if I take a little bitty morsel, that morsel is about the size of the revelation that I receive. If I take a thimble size cup, one tiny taste of a swallow, that again is about the amount of revelation that I receive. I am looking for more of Jesus than that. I don't want to feed my body – I want revelation of Jesus.

What really matters in my day is the Jesus that I see. I have to see Jesus. There isn't anything that I do that is more important than having revelation of Jesus Christ. Religious traditions of men will no longer prevent me from partaking of this great Table of the Lord every day, or as "often" as I want, or need. This is Jesus.

Let us not take up the offensive behavior of continuing to prophesy of brokenness when it was prophesied that "not one bone in His body would be broken." And I am not prophesying a broken body any more. I will declare it to God's people, and God's people aren't going to take the dead religious traditions of men, anymore. God's people are going to see Jesus. They want to see Jesus, and they will, because Jesus is more important to them than a name brand preacher, or a denomination, or a theology, or a philosophy. Jesus Christ is more important to God's people than the favor of religious men.

I have never taught the Table of the Lord the same way twice. This is because there is always more of Jesus. If you partake of Communion multiple times a day for the rest of your life, you still won't get to the end of the revelation of Jesus. But what you will get is better. Instead of being bitter – you will get better, …Better,… and BETTER.

The revelation of Jesus will change you, and you will walk out from under the heavy hand of the taskmaster that has held you down. You will get delivered from your afflictions over and over again. As you partake of His Table, you will keep getting delivered from your afflictions. Yes, many are the afflictions of the righteous, but Jesus came to deliver you from every single one of them. One by one. Ten by ten. A thousand by a thousand. It makes no difference. "God is not restrained to save by many or by few."

Of course, what I am suggesting is that you take a new look at all of this.

The Revelation Of Jesus Christ

The Revelation Of Christ Jesus Will Change The Church

Here are few short stories about the powerful relationship that the church has available through the Table Of The Lord.

In the mid-1990's, I began to share the revelation of The Table Of The Lord in one of our churches in Florida, and there was a sound from heaven that the people heard. It changed the entire ministry of the church. In fact, we ended up having a funeral for the old church. It sounds funny but, yes, we had a literal funeral service for the old church!

They built an actual casket, and on a Saturday afternoon the elders, the pastors, and I gathered together in suits and ties along with a church full of people.

We set the casket right in front of the platform. We put the organizational papers of the old church inside the casket. I conducted the meeting just like a funeral of any person who has passed away. I announced to them all the separations and all of the damages of that particular church body that had occurred through the years. It had been a church of about twenty years, and much had happened during that time. I said ... "Oh, the people that have been broken off from this place ... All the ravaging ... All the bloodshed by the sword of the tongue ... All the members of the body that have been cut off."

Then I said, "We are going to repent. This is a 'river' church. We are going to repent." The Spirit of God came upon that place, and there was weeping that came from the deepest places of the human soul. Oh, it was a powerful thing to experience! I just let it go for a little while, and then I said, "God hears your prayer, and you have repented. It is now time for new life." Then suddenly, came rejoicing. The pallbearers then came and carried the casket outside. We marched right out the back, and the casket was ignited and was burnt completely into ashes. We then renamed the church to The Revival Outreach Center of Hillsborough County.

Communing With The Father

A new baby was born. A baby full of life and joy.

Now, there is a Macaroni Grill Restaurant right near the church, which has been a frequent stopover for many of us. Rick Wilson, the pastor of the Revival Outreach Center, took my armorbearer and me to lunch there one day, and it was there, that we had a bit of a vision. You see, at the Macaroni Grill, they have wine jugs everywhere! It is decorated with wine jugs. It seemed that if there was an empty space anywhere, they put a wine jug in it. So, with this in mind, the church started bringing jugs of grape juice, and they decorated the church with jugs of grape juice and Matzo cracker boxes. Pretty pictures are nice, but they just wanted the revelation of Jesus' body and His Blood. For quite some time, when people would come into that church building they would look around and see jugs of grape juice everywhere. For the next two decades, it was a place where signs and wonders took place, where the revelation of Jesus (Yeshua) was made real to so many, and hearts and lives were changed.

In the church in Florida, there was a lady who's husband was smoking dope and wouldn't come out of the bedroom. He often said nasty things to her and was terribly mean to her. She started partaking of communion in her house. The first time she did this, she declared the Blood of Christ upon the door frames of her house, and she called upon the judging hand of God to come upon that house. While she was revelating on the bloodline and those things that we have been discussing in this book, her husband came out of the bedroom and began to apologize to her for things he said months before! He didn't have a clue what he was doing. This woman is such a believer that she carries a sports cup (like you get at a convenience store) full of grape juice with her in her car. Wherever she goes, she has a cup of juice and a little baggie full of crackers. She is ready to revelate on Jesus because she knows the power of the Table of the Lord!

In the mid-1980's, we founded a church in Renton, Washington, where I continually taught the people about the Table Of The Lord. We moved the church into a district that was noted as a center of satanic activities. We would do what we called "fetish walks" every day around the church and nearly every time we circled the building we would find fetishes that the satanists would place by a door or window or the corners of the building.

Communing With The Father

We often had visitors that were actually satanists that were there to disrupt our services and our lives if possible. This caused what I knew to be a very dangerous atmosphere for the people. So, we would serve the Table Of The Lord in the midst of our service a lot. I would decree the Body and the Blood of Jesus strongly. The innocent Blood of Christ Jesus that was given freely by Him. I would proclaim that satan only steals blood, but the Christ of the Father gave His Blood. Christ's Blood trumps all the other bloods every single time. This would cause the atmosphere to change, and those who were of satan could not get out of that church fast enough.

We understood by facing satanism openly that the Table Of The Lord was our lifeline and our protection, our dome of security against wickedness.

I cannot count the number of times that I've served the Table Of The Lord on lands that have been cursed and witnessed unusual manifestations that are unexplainable either on the lands or somehow connected to the land. Remembering the Lord's death and paying particular attention to the scriptures and what is said about the hill called Golgotha and the lands of Egypt tells us that there is a very close relationship that the Table Of The Lord has with any land.

The Blood of Jesus speaks louder than the blood of Abel. Abel's blood cried out from the land. Golgotha was known as the place of the skull because it was the traditional burial ground of Adam and Eve. That means that the Blood of the last Adam fell to the ground where the first Adam's body turned to dust as the Lord told him it would. That is a powerful restoration of land if you ask me. I have great faith in the Table Of The Lord and its relationship with land and the healing of lands that have been defiled.

Because of the death of the firstborn of every womb that took place on the evening of the first Passover, I consider the inheritance of the believer as something very holy. When there is a miscarriage of a child, I try to bring the mother and father to the Table Of The Lord for the healing of emotions and establish or re-establish the inheritance of them as believers. I consider that the Lamb - the Passover Lamb - Who was Jesus (Yeshua), came from the womb of Mary (Miriam) and how the angel told her that He would deliver the world from sin.

The last statement that Jesus (Yeshua)

made on the cross before He gave up His Spirit from His body was, "Father, into your hands I commit my Spirit." This says that when any loved one dies, we have the individual authority of a believer to commit their spirit into the hands of justice of our heavenly Father. Whether we are speaking of a yet to be born child or an aged person, the person's spirit was given to them by the Father and neither young or old has any measurable difference.

I remember teaching the leaders of our church in Renton, Washington for a week of night meetings on the power of the Body and the Blood of Christ at the Table Of The Lord. The leader of one of our worship teams had several abortions before she had come to know Christ as her savior. One of the night's teaching was on this subject, and we all came to the Table Of The Lord, and I declared the spirit life unto every unborn child and every loved one that was gone into the eternals. At that time, while partaking of the Table Of The Lord, the lady saw herself in a birthing type room, and she saw coming forth from her, every one of the children that she had aborted. The midwife was the Lord Jesus Himself, and He named each of her children and took them away to Himself.

Irene and I did not know that for most of this lady's life she was plagued during her menstrual cycle with unbearable and disabling pain for close to a week. She later reported to us that her next cycle went almost unnoticed to her. Some years later, Irene and I were visiting Renton, Washington and we went to a park and ran into this lady. She was living in California and was also visiting. We asked her if she was still healed and she said, "Oh, yes! What a wonderful miracle night that was for me!"

I've heard it said that familiarity breeds contempt, but I do not believe that to be true. Our very desire for relationship and familiarity seems to be proof that it is not evil to desire close relationships. There is, however, an over-familiarity, or perhaps, inordinate familiarity, that breeds contempt. In other words, familiarity and close relationship must call us to a higher place of honor if we are to enter into a close and familiar relationship with either the Lord or with one another. Honor is the key to healthy relationships.

Becoming familiar with the Father by a deeper and stronger revelation of the Son of God, and the great Table of blessings that He provides is to recognize His power and see it applied to your life. You can come to His Table and have revelation of Him. You can come to His Table and realize, even continually experience, the power of it. But you must come to His Table without religious pretense. Come to His Table, not by habit, or rote exercise - come to His Table and experience the power of the Kingdom of God!

At some point in time, theologians began telling us that ceremony of Communion was an ordinance. An Ordinance is a law. They made it a law because they knew that Jesus wanted us to partake of Communion, but they did not know why. The only thing that they could say is that it is Jesus' law to do so. Thus, we have been robbed of the power that can be experienced at the Table of the Lord. I am sure that when you find deliverance at this Table, you will never be able to approach this Table in the same religious way, and you will never be able to have enough of it. Communion is the revelation of Jesus, and how could you get too much of Jesus? How can you see too much of Him?

Communion ceremonies became law because the meaning and purpose of the individual's life fell away. There is a great command of Yahweh in the book of Deuteronomy, telling all Israel to remember the deliverance of the Lord.

Jesus took the bread and decreed the most powerful metaphor of all time, that this bread was His body.

And likewise with the wine, "this cup is the New Covenant of My Blood." Just as the blood of an innocent lamb had metaphorically stood for the innocent Blood of Jesus Christ, which was to come, now He was giving the apostles and the Ecclesia to come, a metaphor fulfilled by Him which would become the greatest testimony of innocence that could be presented as evidence and would cause the justice of the Creator to respond to every need of deliverance.

In Luke's account of that greatest of Passover evenings, he relates, "And when He had taken some bread and given thanks, He broke and gave to them, saying, "This is My body which is given for you; do this in remembrance of Me." Luke 22:19

When Jesus declared that the apostles should do this in His remembrance, it was not because He simply wanted to be remembered by them. The same is true when the apostle Paul told the Corinthian assembly that they were to "remember the

Lord's death until He comes." This remembrance is to bring up into your memory the testimony of His innocent sacrifice. The testimony of innocence that cries out for justice.

Every Passover is about the great deliverance of Israel from their slavery in Egypt and was being remembered by Yeshua (Jesus) on that spectacular night. Remember. Remember that the Lord delivered Israel. This is the way that we call up the facts of every case of injustice. We call up to memory that God our Father is a God of deliverance. He Who has created all things is just. Jesus is known in all of creation and the heavens and the throne room as the Just. Communion is Passover.

I find it sad that most Christians do not know that Communion is Passover or at least do not know the implications of deliverance in this important fact. The greatest testimony of deliverance that is available to the Ecclesia is that of the Body and the Blood of Jesus, especially how it relates to the precedence of Israel's deliverance from Egyptian slavery.

Now, in my estimation, the duty of the Ecclesia is to bring forth justice from heaven and decree it so that justice might manifest upon the earth. That goes along with mountain moving faith. If the Ecclesia is to present evidence unto the Lord, then it should begin with Passover, Communion, or I prefer calling it the Table Of The Lord.[13]

There is better equity of time if your day begins with the Table of the Lord. You may say that you are too busy to do that, but in reality, you can't afford not to come to His Table today, and every day. What you do with your tomorrow is up to you. If the most important thing is that you see Jesus, then you can do something about it now. Go ahead. See Jesus if you want. He has made a way where there seemingly is no way. He is not hiding from you. He is not hiding His face. He has not silenced His voice from you, so you can both see and hear Him. You can even touch Him. The fact is, you can eat His Flesh and drink His Blood if that is what you want. Now, I call that intimacy.

Now, when partaking of the Table of the Lord with others, please don't condemn folks because they do something different. If they break the body, it is because they don't know any better. This doesn't ruin

---

[13] From "Change The World with Prayer by Wayne C. Anderson; page 91-92

my revelation of the Lord when I come to the Table with those who do so. I know better, and I simply prophesy differently.

It is also important to remember, if you come to the Table of the Lord with someone, and they say, "This is my body broken for you," don't correct them. It is not your job to correct them. Give them this book or wait until they have the apostolic revelation of the freedom of prophesying unity and wholeness.

It is not my intention for anyone to read this book or hear one of my messages on the subject of the Table of the Lord and make a set of rules that will be as harmful as the ones that we have lived under for more than a hundred years. This Table of the Lord is about freedom from the dead religion that hung Jesus on the cross.

It is more important to love than to be right. Why? Because needing to be right only reveals the wrongs of others and is self-righteousness at best. But consider this: Love covers a multitude of sin. You see, love has you covered. So, come to the Table as often as is possible and when others do not have revelation like you, just love them. If you really do have a revelation of the body and Blood of Jesus Christ, then you will love them and not have to be right. You will love them. And, your love will even cover a multitude of sin. Love is the greatest!

Our job is simply to love people. The Table of the Lord is a great doctrine of our faith and needs to be taught with love and with the revelation of the presence of God. His body is His Church! Don't mess with Jesus' body, because that is wrongly discerning the body of Christ. When you start wrongly discerning the body of Christ, and wrongly discerning a "broken" body, then there is more opportunity for many sick to be among us and some may even sleep. We must start discerning this body correctly, with love, and when we do, there is healing in it. There is healing deliverance!

Remembrance of His death by divine revelation will bring about miracles. Though His body was not (and will never be) broken, He was beaten, bruised, and mistreated for you and me, and He wore a crown of thorns to destroy the curse of poverty upon our minds and lives.

Let us run to the Table of the Lord! Let us prophesy of the healing and the deliverance that it was intended to bring. "In the same way, also he took the cup, after supper, saying, 'This cup is the new covenant in my blood. Do this, as often as you drink it, in remembrance of me.' For as often as you eat this bread and drink the cup, you proclaim the Lord 's death until he comes." 1 Corinthians 11:25-26 (ESV)

He said, "I have passionately desired to eat this Passover with you!"

Amen!

The End Is The Beginning At The Father's Table

Ah! Dear reader, we have come through all of the learning stuff, the readjustments of our old understandings of the great and glorious Table of our Father. But now, we can just enjoy His Presence in His House.

What's that? His House you say? Yes, well it was constructed by Him, but it's true that it is actually your house. And, now you probably understand that it is actually your Table. The Father has built this all for you - oh, and me. He doesn't want us to be alone. No, He desires that we are all together in the House that He has constructed for us. Each room is exquisitely furnished to enhance with every nuance the destiny of every individual. Yea, that's impossible, at least from the earthly viewpoint. But, this is not earth. This is your birthplace. This is your family dwelling place.

Everything is different here in a comforting way. The restrictions and restraints are inoperable, and the future has joy-filled expectations.

This adventure has been exciting, and the possibilities of the ways that you might apply what I've taught you is so exhilarating to me. I dream of your new freedom and your attraction to the Table of the revelation of the Lord - Messiah - and the King's Kingdom restored. I mean, that it is now being restored in you, dear reader.

You see, because I believe in the Father, and I believe in His Son, I can also believe in you.

If while you attend His gathering at His Table, you decide to investigate the other rooms and halls and courts of His great house, you'll find intriguing and majestic things that are only privy to the daughters and sons of the Most High.

What do you do with the promises that are here on the Table? Oh, they are your promises of your past, your present, and your future. These are promises that have already adorned your life with delicate and intricate filagree of the Master's artistic and loving nature. You are beautifully accomplished in His eyes. Yet, these are the good times and bad times as you would name them. There are no such things in the Father's House because all things have His perspective and not the earthy view of man. You see, there are not good times or bad times. All are glorious adventures in the elaborate making of a destiny: Your destiny.

He has a design, and every promise is about what you mean to Him. Remember how king David said, "Yea though I walk through the valley of the shadow of death I will fear no evil because You are with me." This was because David knew about the promises that adorn the Master's Table. David was aquatinted with the halls, the rooms, the courts of the Almighty. David knew that the Table was prepared by the Messiah. He tried to make his own palace in the likeness of the House that was constructed by Adonai. David was not satisfied with earthly dwellings because he had seen the House of Yahweh on the nights and the days that he spent tending his father Jesse's flock in the wilderness of Bethlehem. As the king of all Israel, he felt his house could only represent a likeness of Elohim's own House and the dwelling place that would be David's eternal home. David knew.

If David knew, then you, dear reader, can also know. You can be at His Table and see forever and ever. You can come to know the will of the Father from heaven to earth. You have something that no one of this earth can know of or experience. You have a place set at His Table reserved for you. Please understand that this is a great honor for you.

Did the apostles of Yeshua (Jesus) know these things? Well, I'm sure that they didn't know as much as they came to know, through time at the Master's Table. They had to have reflected deeply upon the things the Messiah said at the Table on that spectacular evening in the upper room. But, the meanings evolved into the truth which they taught to the multitudes of hungry people.

What's that you say? Do you have to leave the Table? Ah, that is a common question of those who really partake of the substance of this magnificent adventure. No, you don't have to leave this place. That is why the first believers were declaring the Passover Table at every meal. They never wanted to leave the presence of the Father at His Table.

The End Is The Beginning

Nothing has changed, dear reader, you don't have to leave His majestic Presence at His resplendent Table. You can just carry on with the Table Of The Lord as it was meant to be.

You see, the Table Of The Lord is like the cave of Elijah to you, when it is written that, "behold, a voice came to him and said, 'What are you doing here, Elijah?'" [footnote to 1 Kings 19:13 (NASB)] This was the still, small voice that could only be heard if one was sitting close to the Father of all creation to hear His whisper.

So, hear the very whisper of the Lord, dear reader, and know that He is speaking His loving words to you. Every cry for deliverance is heard and will be answered.

The Table Of The Lord is now meant to be prominent of our spiritual experiences from here on. You are of the age, the era, the kairos, the chronos, the ions, of the Lord. The Table Of The Lord will be that significant place where justice will prevail and your deliverance will come forth like the rain, for "...O sons of Zion, and be glad in the Lord your God; for He has given you the early rain for your vindication. And He has poured down for you the rain, the

Communing With The Father

early and latter rain as before."[14]

Remember, dear reader, how the children of Israel worked as slaves on that one day, yet the evening of a new day began for them, and they feasted together on the Lamb. That evening of the new day was the beginning of their deliverance. They were beginning to know the Father in a new and refreshing way, for they cried to Him, He heard their cry, and He answered them with His deliverance.

"So let us know, let us press on to know the Lord. His going forth is as certain as the dawn; and He will come to us like the rain, like the spring rain watering the earth."[15]

You, my friend, now have the Table Of The Lord. It has now been returned to you from the hands of the controlling, religious and greedy spiritual forces who stole if from the children of God. But it is yours now. Do not let anyone take this Table from you.

Although this book is at the end of its pages, the Father's House and His glorious Table will never leave you. So, please,

---
[14] Joel 2:23 (NASB)
[15] Hosea 6:3 (NASB)

The End Is The Beginning

don't leave Him.

I do hope that you have enjoyed this adventure. I certainly have, for, like the Master, "I have earnestly desired to eat this Passover with you..."

Now, just listen. The Father's whisper can break through the silence and be all that you will ever need.

ABOUT THE AUTHOR

Wayne C Anderson and his wife Irene Joy Anderson live in Meridian, Idaho, the western foothills of the Rocky Mountains. Wayne & Irene met and married in Seattle, Washington, and after near 45 years of marriage, are the delighted parents of 7 children, 15 grandchildren.

While in Seattle, Wayne spent 12 years as a firefighter for the City of Seattle, and for more than 20 years Wayne & Irene pastored in South Seattle. Wayne was the 7th president of the Ministerial Fellowship of the USA, originally founded by John G. Lake. Much of Wayne's ministry has been that of an influential national and international leader. He was one of the principle leaders of Seattle Revival Center, which birthed a revival in the mid 1990's, having also been at the epicenter of revivals in Finland, Mexico, Africa and the US.

Wayne has now established churches and ministries in numerous countries and is the founding Presiding Apostolic Director of International Apostolic Ministries, a fast growing apostolic network.

Wayne & his son Joshua were honorably summoned to appear before the current Sanhedrin in Jerusalem on June 4th, 2013, which was a momentous and life changing experience.

Wayne periodically speaks with governmental leaders in the United States and other nations with an anointed voice of wisdom, which changes the hearts of leaders. He is an in-depth Bible teacher with growing revelatory development toward fathering and miracles and the expansion of our worldview, while he continues to travel the world preaching & equipping believers with keys of the kingdom of God. As an author and speaker, Wayne is diligently working to change the landscape of the Kingdom worldview of believers around the globe.

Get the Book by Wayne C Anderson

Change The World with Prayer

Standsure.net/changetheworld

Available in paperback, large print & Kindle edition
(also available in Español)

Become a ministry Partner with

Wayne C & Irene Joy Anderson

Benefits Of Partnering:

Monthly CD/DVD messages

For Partners Only: Newsletter Monthly Article, Partners' Website, Audio mp3 downloads, Table Of The Lord Videos, Product Discount Coupons, Partner's Podcast

Standsure.net/partner

Join our network family today:

Iamtheway.org

Made in the USA
Columbia, SC
09 July 2018